ANIMAL ARCHITECTS
TERMITES

by Karen Latchana Kenney

Ideas for Parents and Teachers

Pogo Books let children practice reading informational text while introducing them to nonfiction features such as headings, labels, sidebars, maps, and diagrams, as well as a table of contents, glossary, and index.

Carefully leveled text with a strong photo match offers early fluent readers the support they need to succeed.

Before Reading

- "Walk" through the book and point out the various nonfiction features. Ask the student what purpose each feature serves.
- Look at the glossary together. Read and discuss the words.

Read the Book

- Have the child read the book independently.
- Invite him or her to list questions that arise from reading.

After Reading

- Discuss the child's questions. Talk about how he or she might find answers to those questions.
- Prompt the child to think more. Ask: Have you ever seen a mound or another structure made by termites? Did you see the termites building it?

Pogo Books are published by Jump!
5357 Penn Avenue South
Minneapolis, MN 55419
www.jumplibrary.com

Library of Congress Cataloging-in-Publication Data

Names: Kenney, Karen Latchana, author.
Title: Termites / by Karen Latchana Kenney.
Description: Minneapolis, MN: Jump!, Inc., [2018]
Series: Animal architects | Audience: Ages 7-10.
Includes bibliographical references and index.
Identifiers: LCCN 2016054977 (print)
LCCN 2016058900 (ebook)
ISBN 9781620316979 (hardcover: alk. paper)
ISBN 9781624965746 (ebook)
Subjects: LCSH: Termites–Juvenile literature.
Termites–Habitations–Juvenile literature.
Classification: LCC QL529 .K385 2018 (print)
LCC QL529 (ebook) | DDC 595.7/36–dc23
LC record available at https://lccn.loc.gov/2016054977

Editor: Kirsten Chang
Book Designer: Michelle Sonnek
Photo Researchers: Kirsten Chang & Michelle Sonnek

Photo Credits: Piotr Naskrecki/Minden Pictures, cover; Pan Xunbin/Shutterstock, cover; Volodymyr Burdiak/Shutterstock, 1; Piotr Naskrecki/Getty, 3, 23; Ingo Arndt/Nature Picture Library, 4, 5; wonderisland/Shutterstock, 6-7; smuay/Thinkstock, 8-9; imageBROKER/SuperStock, 10; jlarrumbe/Shutterstock, 11; Greentellect_Studio/Thinkstock, 12-13; Satoshi Kuribayashi/Minden Pictures, 14-15; Konrad Wothe/SuperStock, 16-17; bruceman/iStock, 18; Amy Walters/Shutterstock, 19; K Jayaram/Science Photo Library, 20-21.

Printed in the United States of America at Corporate Graphics in North Mankato, Minnesota.

TABLE OF CONTENTS

CHAPTER 1

ARCH BUILDERS

Deep inside their **nest**, tiny white termites work. They are building **arches** in the dark. Each one carries a small ball of mud mixed with their waste.

An arch begins as two pillars.
A termite sticks a ball onto a pillar.
More termites add balls. Soon the
pillars curve in to make an arch.
Arches connect to make domes.
Domed **chambers** make up the nest.

soldier

worker

queen

The nest is home to a **colony**. It is made up of thousands of termites. Each has a special job.

Many are workers. They are the builders. They have small, pale bodies and thin skin. They are also blind. They communicate using a smell that their bodies make.

Soldiers defend the colony. Some have large heads with strong jaws. Others have a tube on their heads. They spray a harmful liquid.

A very large queen only lays eggs. She may lay up to 30,000 eggs a day.

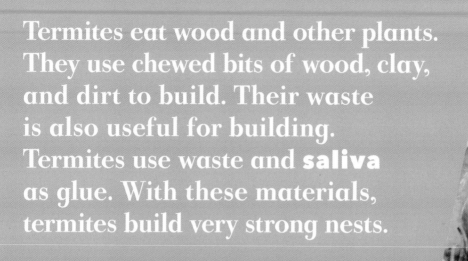

Termites eat wood and other plants. They use chewed bits of wood, clay, and dirt to build. Their waste is also useful for building. Termites use waste and **saliva** as glue. With these materials, termites build very strong nests.

DID YOU KNOW?

Some termites are farmers. They grow a **fungus** on their waste. Then they eat the fungus and the waste.

CHAPTER 2

MOUNDS AND NESTS

Some termites make their nests inside wood. Others make nests on trees.

But the biggest structures termites build are giant **mounds** out of dirt. Some mounds are taller than a giraffe!

ventilation shaft

Mounds are built above the termites' nest. The colony can make a lot of heat. The mound helps keep the nest at the right temperature.

The mound houses several **ventilation** shafts. There is one central shaft. Smaller shafts branch off from it, leading to small holes in the outside of the mound. Warm, stale air rises and leaves the nest. Fresh, cool air sinks into the nest.

Below the mound is the nest. It has many chambers. They hold the food supply, such as fungus. They hold the queen, **king**, and young termites.

fungus · · · · ▶

TAKE A LOOK!

What does the inside of a termite mound look like?

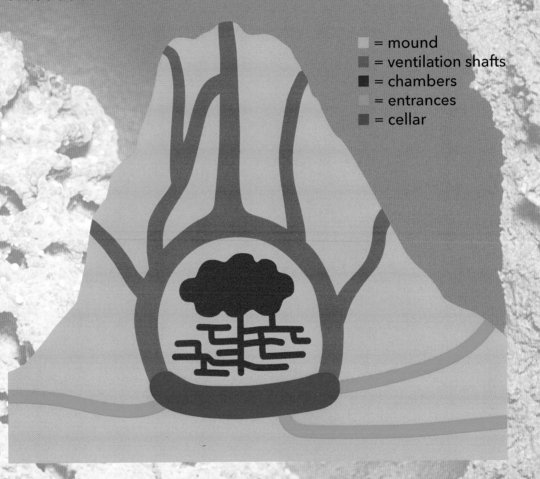

- ☐ = mound
- ☐ = ventilation shafts
- ■ = chambers
- ☐ = entrances
- ■ = cellar

Some termites make their nests in trees. They build a round nest made of **carton**. This is a mix of waste and small bits of wood. It's a little like cardboard. Inside are small rooms called cells.

They build tubes made of carton along the length of the tree. This lets them travel to and from the nest.

CHAPTER 3

TERMITES IN NATURE

Some termites live inside wood. They dig long tunnels. These kinds of termites damage homes. House walls can crumble and break.

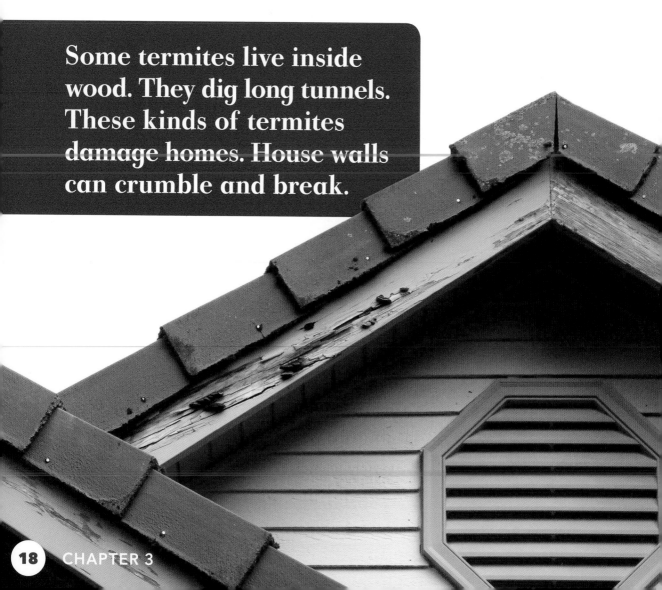

They can also **infest** trees. Their tunnels can weaken wood. Trees may fall down.

Termites are not always harmful. They break down plants and wood. This returns **nutrients** to the soil. Their waste feeds the soil, too. This helps new plants grow. And other animals make their nests in termite mounds. Some lizards lay their eggs inside the mounds to keep them safe.

Making new structures and fixing old ones, tiny termites are always building.

ACTIVITIES & TOOLS

TRY THIS!

SINKING AND RISING AIR

How do termites cool their nests? Watch how temperature makes water move, just like air in a termite nest.

What You Need:
- clear plastic tub
- water
- small plastic bottle
- ice cube tray
- blue and red food coloring

❶ Add blue food coloring to some water. Fill up an ice cube tray with the blue water. Freeze overnight. This will be like the cool air in a termite nest.

❷ Fill the plastic tub with water. Let it sit out overnight.

❸ Ask an adult for help with this step. Fill the small bottle with hot water. Add red food coloring. This will be like the hot air in a termite nest.

❹ Drop a blue ice cube into the tub of room temperature water.

❺ Float the bottle with the red, hot water in the tub. Leave the cap off so some red water spills into the room temperature water.

❻ What happens to the blue ice cube as it melts? The cool blue water sinks, just like cool air. The hot red water floats on top, just like hot air.

GLOSSARY

arches: Curved structures that help support larger structures, such as nests.

carton: Material made by termites that is like paper or cardboard.

chambers: Large rooms.

colony: A large group of insects that live together.

fungus: An organism that does not have leaves, flowers, or fruits, such as a mushroom.

infest: When large numbers of insects are in a certain place.

king: A male termite in the colony that mates with the queen.

mounds: Hills or piles.

nest: A place built by animals and insects to have their young and live in.

nutrients: Substances that are essential for living things to survive and grow.

saliva: A clear liquid in the mouth.

ventilation: A system or means of providing fresh air.

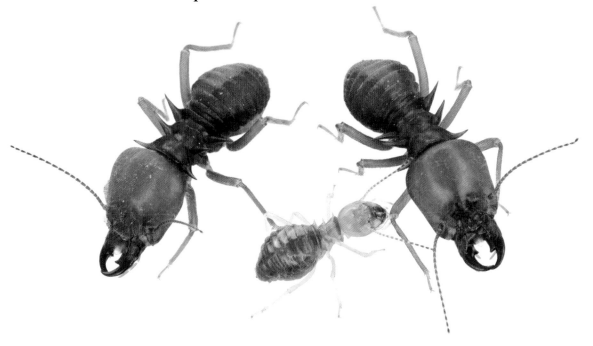

INDEX

TO LEARN MORE

Learning more is as easy as 1, 2, 3.

1) Go to www.factsurfer.com

2) Enter "termitearchitects" into the search box.

3) Click the "Surf" button to see a list of websites.

With factsurfer, finding more information is just a click away.